Let's look at
Animals

Barbara Hunter

Heinemann
LIBRARY

www.heinemann.co.uk/library

Visit our website to find out more information about **Heinemann Library** books.

To order:

☎ Phone 44 (0) 1865 888066

🖹 Send a fax to 44 (0) 1865 314091

💻 Visit the Heinemann Bookshop at www.heinemann.co.uk/library to browse our catalogue and order online.

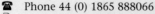

First published in Great Britain by Heinemann Library,
Halley Court, Jordan Hill, Oxford
OX2 8EJ, part of Harcourt Education.
Heinemann is a registered trademark of Harcourt
Education Ltd.

Editorial: Jilly Attwood and Claire Throp
Design: Jo Hinton-Malivoire and bigtop,
Bicester, UK
Models made by: Jo Brooker
Picture Research: Catherine Bevan
Production: Lorraine Warner

Originated by Dot Gradations
Printed and bound in China by South China Printing
Company

ISBN 0 431 16382 0 (hardback)
06 05 04 03 02
10 9 8 7 6 5 4 3 2 1

ISBN 0 431 16387 1 (paperback)
06 05 04 03 02
10 9 8 7 6 5 4 3 2 1

British Library Cataloguing in Publication Data
Hunter, Barbara
Let's Look at Animals
704.9'432
A full catalogue record for this book is available from
the British Library.

Acknowledgements
The publishers would like to thank the following for
permission to reproduce photographs:
AKG London pp. **7**, **11**; AKG London, © ADAGP, Paris
And DACS, London 2002 p. **15**; Ancient Art And
Architecture Collection Library p. **4**; Christian
Pierre/Superstock p.**14**; Copyright 2002 Board Of
Trustees, National Gallery Of Art, Washington p. **23**;
Corbally Stourton Contemporary Art, London, UK/
Bridgeman Art Library p.**16**; Graphische Sammlung
Albertina, Vienna, Austria/ Bridgeman Art Library p.**13**;
Kunstmuseum, Dusseldorf, Germany/Bridgeman Art
Library p.**12**; Mallett & Son Antiques Ltd., London,
UK/Bridgeman Art Library p.**19**; Musee Picasso, Paris,
France/Bridgeman Art Library, © Succession
Picasso/DACS 2002 p. **9**; Museum Of Cycladic And
Ancient Greek Art, Athens, Greece/Bridgeman Art
Library p.**18**; National Gallery, London, UK/Bridgeman
Art Library, © Succession Picasso/ DACS 2002 pp. **20/
21**; On Loan To The Hamburg Kunsthalle, Hamburg,
Germany/Bridgeman Art Library, © ADAGP, Paris And
DACS, London 2002 p. **8**; Private Collection/Bridgeman
Art Library p. **5**; Roy Miles Fine Paintings/Bridgeman Art
Library p. **6**; © Succession H Matisse/DACS 2002 p. **22**;
The Henry Moore Foundation p.**10**; Werner Forman
Archive p. **17**.

Cover photograph reproduced with permission of
Bridgeman Art Library/private collection.

The publishers would like to thank Annie Davy for her
assistance in the preparation of this book.

Every effort has been made to contact copyright holders
of any material reproduced in this book. Any omissions
will be rectified in subsequent printings if notice is
given to the publishers.

Contents

Animals

Many artists have painted and carved animals. Even cavemen painted animals.

Noah's Crazy Ark by Maylee Yabar-Davila (1999)

How many different animals can you see in this painting?

Pets

Can you see this kitten's whiskers?
They were painted with a tiny brush.

6

Miss Ann White's Kitten by George Stubbs (1790)

This picture of a dog is called a mosaic. It is made from little pieces of tile.

On the farm

Have you ever been to a farm? Have you seen an animal like this one before?

Red Cow by Jean Dubuffet (1943)

The artist has made this goat out of a metal called bronze.

9

The Goat by Pablo Picasso (1950)

Pigs and sheep

The artist made these sheep sculptures out of bronze. The sheep are in a big field with real sheep.

Sheep Piece by Henry Moore (1962-63)

10

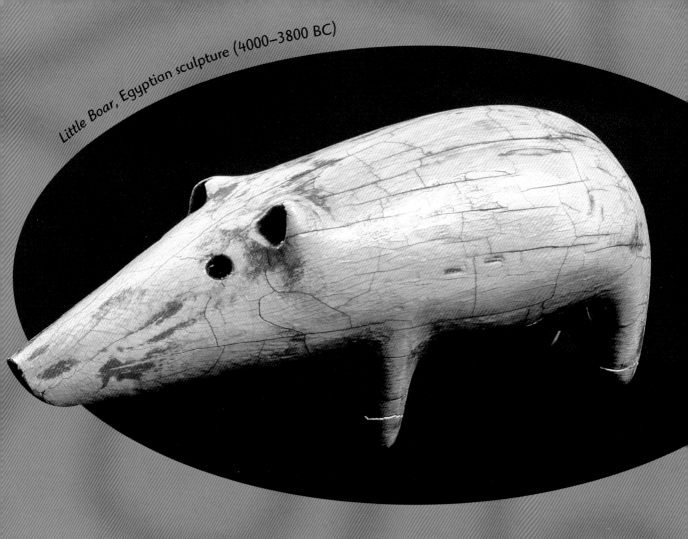

This is a very old sculpture of a pig.
It was made thousands of years ago.

11

In the wild

Can you see the fox's head?

The Fox by Franz Marc (1913)

In this chalk drawing you can see every line and wrinkle in the elephant's skin.

Which of these animals might live in the wild in this country?

Tigers

Tiger by Victor Vasarely (1938)

Can you find a tiger in this pattern?

Has the artist
used colours like
a real tiger?

Young Tiger by Christian Pierre (20th Century)

Snakes

Can you find
the snake in
this picture?

Snake Dreaming by Keith Kaapa Tjangala (1989)

The painting has been made
from lots of coloured dots.

16

This snake has two heads! It has been made from lots of little bits of tiles.

Aztec ornament worn by high priest

Fish

Plate depicting two fish, Greek (350 BC)

18

Fish have been painted onto this ceramic plate.

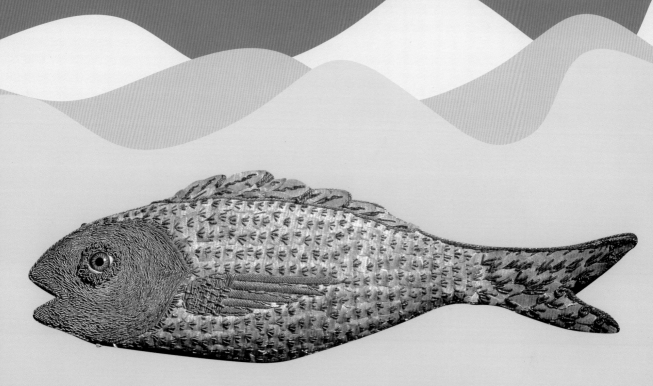

This fish has been made
from shells and gold thread.

Venetian fish (1760)

19

Birds

This girl is holding a bird called a dove.

Can you see any feathers or just the shape?

Picasso

In the garden

This frog has been made from bronze. Do you think it would feel **slimy** like a real frog?

A frog, Paduan (16th century)

22

The Snail by Henri Matisse (1953)

How many coloured pieces
of paper has the artist
used to make this snail?

23

Index

The end

Notes for adults

This series covers the creative development area of learning. Each book looks at works of art from different cultures and different media. This set of books will support the young child's learning about the world around them and provide opportunities for them to explore different types of art. The following key Early Learning Goals are relevant to this series:
• explore colour, texture, shape, form and space in two or three dimensions
• respond in a variety of ways to what they see, hear, smell, touch and feel
• use their imagination in art and design.

Lets Look at Animals includes pictures of animals depicted in different ways. Some are painted and appear very life-like and some are abstract and appear as a 'pattern' (see 'Tigers' p14). Some techniques will need to be explained to the children.

Children will need to explore the differences between a 2-D painting and a 3-D sculpture and it will be necessary to explain that some artists represent their work in a literal way, like a photograph, while some paint or draw how an object 'feels' to them so it may not look like the 'real thing'. Discussing how some objects make children feel, or what they are reminded of when they see them, can help understanding.

Key vocabulary that can be explored through this book includes *painted, carved, tiny, brush, metal, sculpture, artist, drawing, chalk, pattern, colours, ceramic* and *spiral*.

Follow-up activities
Children could make a clay or plasticine model of a pig or a snake and contrast their shapes and the skills needed to make them. It would obviously be beneficial to have seen some of the animals first hand, and a visit to a farm or aquatic centre will help with their artistic interpretations of the animals.

24